# Pondering & Forming Jesus in Our Hearts

Selected Homilies And Reflections For
The Liturgical Season Of Advent
( A,B,C )

FR. AZAM VIANNEY MANSHA, CJM
EUDIST PRIEST - MISSIONARY OF MERCY

ISBN: 978-1-959312-30-7

Copyright ©2025, by
The Eudists – CJM, Inc.
All Rights Reserved.

Published by

PO Box 3619
Vista, CA 92085
www.eudistsusa.org

# Dedication

To my departed family members
Who played a significant role in my life

### Great - grandmother

Veera Mughal Bibi

### Grandparents

Sharif Mughal & Meera Bibi

Bashir (Kala) Masih
[grandfather's younger brother]

Sharifa Bibi
[maternal grandmother]

### Father

Mansha Sharif

### Brothers and sisters

Amjad John Mansha

Salomi Amin [first cousin]

Noman Amin [First cousin]

Daniel Safdar [First cousin]

### Uncle and Aunties

Amin Sharif

Safia Mansha Sharif Bibi

Jamilia Lazar Nawab Bibi
[maternal aunty]

# Contents

**The Solemnity of Our Lord Jesus Christ, King of the Universe (A)** ............... 5

– Are you a Giver or Self-absorbed!?! (A)

**First Sunday of Advent (A, B & C)** ......... 13

– Putting on the Armor of the Light (A)

– WATCH: Your Words + Actions + Thoughts = Christ in your Hearts (B)

– Detaching from Worldly Pleasures in Order to Attach to Divine Graces (C)

**Second Sunday of Advent (B)** ................. 35

– New Exodus + Humility = Promised Heaven (B)

**Third Sunday of Advent "*Gaudete Sunday*" (A & B)** .......................................... 43

- Arrival of the Holy One of Israel Among Us! (A)

- Rejoice and Pray without Ceasing (B)

**Fourth Sunday of Advent (A, B, C) ........ 57**

- Through a Virgin, the Savior has entered into the World (A)

- New Davidic Kingdom (B)

- The Twofold Gifts of Mary's Greetings (C)

**The Solemnity of the Nativity of the Lord, "Christmas" (B) ............................. 83**

- Bethlehem + Manger = Jesus, the Divine Bread

**The Feast of the Holy Family of Jesus, Mary and Joseph (B) ............................. 91**

- Obedience + Love = Salvation - Jesus Christ

**The Solemnity of the Blessed Virgin Mary, the Mother of God (A)** ............... 99

— To Jesus through Mary

**About Saint John Eudes** ...................... 109

**About the Eudist Family** ...................... 115

**About the Author** ............................... 120

# Back story

During my "Special Year of Eudist Formation" in the Philippines, I had the pleasure of meeting different Eudist priests from around the world. One of them was Fr. Pierre Drouin, CJM (former General Superior of the Eudists and Eudist missionary to Venezuela), who continuously emphasized the urgency of preparing and preaching fruitful homilies as a way "to form Jesus" in others. Although his words were simple, they deeply penetrated my heart. The Eudist spirituality was then integrated into my very being.

St. John Eudes (1601- 1608) was known for his preaching. He preached and celebrated the sacraments at 117 parish missions, for months at a time. In one of his letters (letter no. 75), he wrote:

> I have not preached in the church for quite some time now, for although it is very large, it nevertheless is too small on this occasion. I can truthfully say that

we have more than fifteen thousand people present on Sundays.

There are twelve confessors, but without exaggeration, there is enough work for fifty. People come from a distance of eight or ten leagues [16 to 20 miles], and their hearts are so touched that there is nothing to be seen but tears and nothing to be heard but laments from the poor penitent men and women.

As a spiritual son of St. John Eudes, I have been blessed to be part of a rich tradition of "forming Jesus in hearts" through preaching the Word of God with zeal and compassion. This book is a fruit of my preaching ministry in the Philippines and in the United States of America. I am grateful to the Lord, who called this sinner from the ends of the world to proclaim His Word around the world.

I must confess that during this journey of preaching, God has blessed me with three different editors: Lolly Roxas, Donna Edwin and Cece Haynor.

During my stay in the Philippines, Lolly Roxas edited my homilies and other works. I am greatly indebted to her for the tireless service which she rendered to me, her spiritual son. Aside from this, the Roxas family (Jack, Lolly, Katya, Mia & Kaylie) became my family-away-from-family. They were constantly visiting me during the Covid-19 pandemic, and they helped me establish the Eudist Food Pantry, which served 200 families every week for more than a year in the Philippines.

When I transferred to San Diego, California, Donna Edwin graciously volunteered to become my editor and edited my weekly homilies.

Cece is another blessing from the Lord. Bill, her husband, was the one who told me that Cece is a good editor. Indeed, she is a good editor. Cece edited my previous book, "*To Jesus Through Mary*" as well as this current book.

Lastly, I would like to extend my gratitude to our Eudist staff, Steve Marshall and Ralda Rizke. What you are holding in your hands is actually the hard work of Steve Marshall, who did all the necessary technical work so that this book could be published by the Eudist Press and also be available on Amazon. Ralda, on the other hand, has provided her expertise to make sure that you get a copy in your hands.

  I pray, hope and believe that this current collection of Advent homilies (from 2021 to 2024) and reflections will help you to ponder and form Jesus in your hearts during the busy and festive season of Advent and Christmas.

# The Solemnity of Our Lord Jesus Christ, King of the Universe (A)

> Ez 34:11-12, 15-17; Ps 23:1-3, 5-6;
> 1 Cor 15:20-26, 28 & Mt 25:31-46

**Are you A Giver or Self-absorbed!?!**

Dear sisters and brothers in Christ,

We have reached the climax of the Liturgical Year (A) with the Solemnity of Christ the King, also known as the Solemnity of Our Lord Jesus Christ, King of the Universe. To mark the conclusion of Matthew's Chapter 25, today we have a third parable known as "The Parable of the Judgment of Nations." I still have fresh memories about leaving the Philippines to come to San Diego. I received a wonderful *Despedida* (a going-away party) from Turning the Bible Pages with the Eudists - the Bible group which I founded during

COVID. We met online every week to deepen our spiritual understating of the Sunday readings. During the *Despedida* celebration, the Master of Ceremonies, Ms. Lolly Roxas, asked a question of the participants, "What is Fr. Azam's favorite Bible passage?" Not one, but everyone, shouted, "Matthew 25:31-45," and then they started singing:

> Whatsoever you do to the least of my people
> That you do unto me.
>
> When I was hungry, you gave me to eat;
> When I was thirsty, you gave me to drink.
> Now enter into the home of my Father.
>
> Whatsoever you do to the least of my people
> That you do unto me.

I got very emotional! As I am now!!! Indeed, this is not only my favorite Bible passage, but it is our Christian vocation; it is the commandment of the Lord; and it is our preparation for the judgment. What I actually would like to propose for today's spiritual journey are only two points: the criteria of judgment and the presence of Jesus.

Prior to deepening our understanding about the current Gospel passage, I would like to briefly state that this Gospel passage does not only highlight the criteria of judgment, but it helps us to understand that there is an end of the world. In this way, there will be judgment, which means that some will be asked to enter into the kingdom of God and some, unfortunately, will be sent to eternal fire. Consider the following passage:

> When the Son of man comes in his glory ... all the nations will be assembled before him ... And he will separate them one from another ... Then the king will say to those on his right, *"come ... Inherit the kingdom prepared for you* ... Then he will say to those on his left, *'Depart from me you accursed into the eternal fire prepared for the devil and his angels ..."*
> Mt 25:31-46 (emphasis added)

Therefore, I believe this would be a wonderful Gospel passage to meditate on for those people who do not believe in eternal life and eternal fire.

With this in mind, let's move on to the criteria of judgment. The close reading of the Gospel passage shows two groups of people, namely, the givers and the self-absorbed. As the parable goes on, you can see that both groups of people were not judged based on their belief or profession of faith, but they were judged by their actions. Let's quickly look at the group of givers or doers who went out of their way to feed the hungry, to offer water to the thirsty, to accommodate the stranger, to clothe the naked, and to visit the sick and the prisoners. They gave and loved others without looking for a reward; they did it without being told; therefore, they were surprised and said, "When did we see you hungry, thirsty, naked, a stranger, sick or a prisoner?" This group of givers saw the need and addressed it without looking for a reward or waiting for instructions.

On the other hand, the group of self-absorbed people did not perform any action when there was a need to feed the hungry, to offer water to the thirsty, to clothe the naked, to accommodate the stranger and to visit the sick and the prisoners. They were so much into themselves or self-absorbed that they did not see the needs of others. Consequently, the Father did not punish the self-absorbed group because they were adulterers, murderers, robbers or of any other type of mortal sinners, but the Father punished them for not doing anything for the "least brothers and sisters" among us, because God lives among the needy and the poor.

With this, we move on to the second and final point of today's reflection, which is, the real presence of Jesus. Through the Sacred Scripture we have learned that Jesus lives among us or is present among us in two different ways, namely, 1. in the sacraments; and 2. in the needy and the poor. The most profound example we can cite is the Holy Eucharist, where Jesus is fully present and among us, as He, Himself, told the Apostles at the Last Supper, "THIS IS MY BODY." Also, at the breaking of the bread at Emmaus, the disciples were reminded by Jesus that He is fully present in the bread.

The second way Jesus is living among us is through the needy and the poor around us, as He, Himself, associates with them, by stating, "Amen, I say to you, whatever you DID for one of the least brothers of mine, you DID for ME" and "Amen, I say to you, what you DID NOT DO for one of these least ones, you DID NOT DO for ME." In that way, we have a two-fold presence of Jesus, which is through the sacraments and through the poor. Therefore, we nourish the soul through the sacraments to get strength to serve the poor, who are the brothers and sisters of Jesus Christ.

Dear sisters and brothers of Christ, let's not forget the words of St. Jeanne Jugan (Foundress of the Little Sisters of the Poor -1792-1879), a spiritual daughter of St. John Eudes, who said, ". . . never forget that the poor are Our Lord; in caring for the poor say to yourself: "This is for my JESUS . . .!" And she also said, "Look upon the poor with compassion, and Jesus will look kindly upon you on your last day."

May the powerful intercession of the Blessed Mother be our strength to encounter Jesus Christ by feeding the hungry, offering drink to the thirsty, clothing the naked, accommodating the stranger and visiting the sick and prisoners.

# Reflect and Journal

# First Sunday of Advent (A)

> Isa 2:1-5; Ps 122:1-9,
> Rom 13:11-14 & Mt 24:37-44

## Putting on the Armor of the Light

Dear sisters and brothers in Christ,

The Gospel according to St. Matthew has five big sections, and with no surprise, today's Gospel passage has come from the fifth and last section of the Gospel. In other words, we begin our new liturgical year with the end of the Gospel according to St. Matthew. As we unlock the mystery of today's Gospel passage, I would like to emphasize that today's Gospel is not about a secret rapture in which believers will be mysteriously taken into heaven. Indeed, the Gospel passage speaks about final judgment and preparation.

You must have heard the expression that "we win by losing." The end of times or the end of the world does not mean that there is no hope or uncertainty in the next world, but in reality, Jesus is already indicating that losing here our worldly pleasures or things moves us to attain heaven, that is, we win heaven by losing the world. In order to enter into heaven, Jesus used the image of Noah's Ark.

Noah, a man of God, listened to the Lord with his heart, whereas other people were busy with their affairs. Noah prepared himself according to the instructions of the Lord, which not only saved his life, but his act of preparation saved thousands of other creatures. Through the metaphor of Noah and his preparation, Jesus emphasized the importance of preparation, so we can enter in the Ark of God that is the Mother Church, to prepare ourselves to accept the Son of Man.

To begin our preparation in order to welcome the Son of Man, St. Paul gives us moral and spiritual instructions. He encourages the community of believer to "put on the armor of light." This metaphorical expression, "putting on the armor of light," stands for getting ready for a new day.

First and foremost, a question can be asked, "What is the armor of light?" It is "the breastplate of faith and love, and the helmet of hope of salvation" (Thessalonians 5:1-11). So we can understand through St. Paul's expression, "putting on the armor of light," that it is not a simple preparation, but there is something extra-ordinary going on. During war, breastplate, sword and helmet were used by soldiers of war. Indeed, the first Sunday of Advent for us is a call to get ready for spiritual battle, while by putting on the breastplate of faith and hope and the helmet of salvation.

For spiritual battle, the first instructions come from Jesus, Himself, who said, "stay awake" (Matthew 24:42), that is, "be aware" that you are in a spiritual battle. Once again St. Paul helps us to understand how we can "stay awake." He gives a list for staying awake: conduct yourselves properly, that is, respect our bodies; no orgies and drunkenness, that is, control our appetites; no promiscuity and lust, that is, sexual immorality; and no rivalry and jealousy, that is, respect the rights of neighbors. Indeed, during his ministry,

Jesus, Himself, gave a list of sins which defile a person because they come from the heart:

> [Jesus said] For out of the heart come evil intentions, *murder, adultery, sexual immorality, theft, false witness, slander.*
> Matthew 15:19
> (emphasis added)

Dear sisters and brothers, the first Sunday of Advent is a call for us to prepare ourselves by "putting on armor of light," that is, Jesus Christ, so that we can walk in Jesus' light to shine in the world. I believe you know this Christian song - Christ, be our Light! Let's sing together as we begin our journey of Advent together:

> Longing for light, we wait in darkness.
> Longing for truth, we turn to you.
> Make us your own, your holy people,
> Light for the world to see.
>
> **Chorus**
> Christ, be our light!
> Shine in our hearts.

Shine through the darkness.
Christ, be our light!
Shine in your church gathered today.

May Mary, the mother of Jesus and our mother, intercede for us to prepare ourselves while staying awake, in order to put on the armor of light for the spiritual battle, in order to enter into heaven.

# Reflect and Journal

# First Sunday of Advent (B)

> Is 63:16B-17, 19B; 64:2-7; Ps 80:2-3, 15-16, 18-19; 1 Cor 1:3-9 & Mk 13:33-37

## WATCH
## Words + Actions + Thoughts = Christ in Your Hearts

Dear sisters and brothers in Christ,

A blessed and happy New Liturgical Year (B). Let's take a moment to thank the Lord for the previous year's blessings of family members and friends. We should also keep our loved ones who have gone before us in our prayers to glorify the Lord. With this New Liturgical Year B, we are going to journey together to deepen our spiritual understanding and encounter Jesus through the Gospel according to St. Mark. Actually, this week I would like to journey with you to unpack the mystery of "WATCH." The word "watch" actually appears four times in today's Gospel passage, and we will explore together what it actually means. Prior to that, I would like to quickly walk with you to give an overview of the four weeks of Advent in a thematic way:

1. The FIRST WEEK of Advent's Gospel highlights the end of the world;
2. The SECOND WEEK of Advent's Gospel points out the beginning of Jesus' ministry;
3. The THIRD WEEK of Advent's Gospel invites us to see Jesus through the witness of John the Baptist; and
4. The FOURTH WEEK of Advent's Gospel helps us to hear the Good News about the Birth of Jesus in the form of the "Annunciation to Mary."

Let's begin with the FIRST WEEK of Advent's Gospel passage. You might be wondering, the Church is beginning a new year, but we are reading from almost the end of the Gospel (Mk 13:33-37). In other words, Jesus proclaims about the end of the world. In fact, it is the last teaching of Jesus prior to His Passion which began in Jerusalem; a mystery between the end of the world and the beginning of the Advent Season in Holy Mother Church. This theme is so important that the Mother Church is constantly reminding the community of believers about it.

I would like to quickly remind you and advise you - NOT TO PAY ANY ATTENTION to those Gospel prosperity preachers of fear, who present themselves as even higher than JESUS. They are not preachers of prosperity, but they are preachers of fear, while focusing on the end of the world by giving false timelines. If they give timelines about the end of the world, understand immediately that the teaching is not from Jesus Christ, because Jesus, Himself, said in the Gospel according to St. Matthew 24:36, ". . . about that day [the end of the world] and hour no one knows, *neither the angels of heaven, nor the Son*, but only the Father." (I would encourage you to read the whole Chapter 24 of the Gospel according to St. Matthew).

If Jesus does not know about the end of the world and the angels don't know about the end of the world, then how can the prosperity preachers know about the end of the world? Or how can those movie directors know with such productions as "Left Behind," "2012," "The Day After Tomorrow," "The Book of Eli," and "The Rapture?" It seems that their only purpose is to promote fear and empty your pockets in the name of giving away worldly material!!! Therefore, the only thing Jesus told the community of believes about His Second Coming was to "watch." What we actually need to watch is:

W - Words
A - Actions
T - Thoughts - to accept
C - Christ - in your
H - Heart

In this season of Advent, let's begin to watch our words, because sometimes our words can hurt others in the form of gossiping or character assassination. Instead of using discouraging words for others, let's start using the Words of Jesus to uplift others. Let's bring the kind words of Jesus to our wounded society in order for them, as well as for us, to prepare for the Second Coming of Jesus.

Not only with our words, but with actions, let us heal the world. I believe you still remember the Gospel passage from the previous week in which Jesus associated Himself with the hungry, the naked, the thirsty, the sick, the strangers and the prisoners (the Christian song, "Whatsoever you do, to the Least of my People, that you do unto ME . . ." Matthew 25). It is through the eyes of faith that we can see Jesus in the least of our society, and through our actions of mercy and prayers that we can serve them.

We can serve them not only through words and actions, but also through our thoughts. It is very essential and valuable to carry Christ in our thoughts, because it makes us blessed/happy, as the Psalmist says, "Blessed are those who meditate on the Law of the LORD day and night . . ." (paraphrasing the verses - Psalm 1:1-2).

In this Holy Season of Advent, let's bring our whole attention through words, actions and thoughts to Christ, who wants to live in our hearts. I believe you know the prayer which is attributed to St. Patrick, the Patron Saint of Ireland, as well as of our parish in Carlsbad, California, to keep Jesus Christ in our words, actions and thoughts. Let us sing together:

1. Christ be beside me
Christ be before me,
Christ be behind me,
King of my heart;
Christ be within me,
Christ be below me,
Christ be above me
never to part.

2. Christ on my right hand,
Christ on my left hand,
Christ all around me
shield in the strife;
Christ in my sleeping,
Christ in my sitting,
Christ in my rising
light of my life.

May the powerful intercession of the Blessed Ever-Virgin Mary prepare us to WATCH for the Second Coming of Jesus Christ among us.

## Reflect and Journal

# First Sunday of Advent (C)

> Jer 33:14-16; Ps 25:4-5, 8-9, 10, 14; 1 Thes 3:12-4:2 & Lk 21:25-28, 34-36

## Detaching from Worldly Pleasures in order to Attach to Divine Graces

Dear sisters and brothers in Christ,

Happy and blessed new Liturgical Year (C). The Holy Mother invites us to begin this new year to grow in holiness and encounter Jesus Christ. Our new liturgical year is dedicated to the Gospel according to St. Luke. Throughout this liturgical year, most of the time we will be listening to the Gospel according to St. Luke, except on those Sundays when Holy Mother Church wants to highlight the Divinity of Jesus, and shifts from the Gospel according to Luke to the Gospel according to John.

What is Advent? The Latin *adventus* stands for "coming" or "arrival" of the long awaiting Messiah. In Holy Mother Church, Advent is a liturgical season of four weeks, which invites the community of believers to dedicate themselves to anticipating the arrival of the long-awaited Messiah - the Savior of the universe.

There are six liturgical seasons:

1. Advent: First Sunday of Advent through December 24th
2. Christmas: December 25th through the Feast of the Baptism of the Lord
3. Ordinary Time after the Baptism: Monday after the Feast of the Baptism of the Lord through Shrove Tuesday
4. Lent: Ash Wednesday through Holy Saturday
5. Easter: Easter Vigil through Pentecost, and
6. Ordinary Time after Pentecost: The day after Pentecost through the final day before Advent.

On the First Sunday of Advent, you will be surprised that the Gospel passage is almost entirely taken from the end of Jesus' ministry. It is one of those passages known as the eschatological passages in which Jesus talks about the end of times and His second coming (*parousia*). To unpack the Gospel passage, I would like to invite you to journey together to deepen our understanding while reflecting on 3 things: 1. Understanding the effect of sin; 2. Pleasure of this world (*merimna*); and 3. Stay awake and pray. So let's begin first with the third point, that is "stay awake and pray."

Staying awake and praying in the night is a most ancient Jewish practice. For example, see the Psalmist who said, "*At midnight I rise to praise you*, because of your righteous ordinances" (Psalm 119:62 - emphasis added). This ancient practice was/is widely practiced, particularly on the evening of Passover. The Jews on Passover stay up into the night and pray all night. The reason behind this ancient practice is the Jewish tradition that the Messiah would come on the night of the

Passover. Therefore, a person who is waiting for the Messiah must stay awake and pray.

Here Jesus Christ not only instructs His followers, but He reveals His Messianic secret that the way to welcome the Messiah is to stay awake and pray. One should ask, "What does it mean - to stay awake and pray?" Is Jesus telling us not to sleep? NO! To stay awake and pray is a form of disciplining our bodies. Think for a moment! Abstinence from food brings a discipline in body to say no to worldly food in order get ready to receive spiritual food. The spiritual fathers described the pious practice of fasting as detachment from this world's pleasure in order to attach to heavenly graces. Now, abstinence from food means moderately eating and sacrificing the pleasures of food. So in this same manner, when Jesus says, "Stay awake and pray," it is to bring moderation into our sleep. It is a form of detachment from the pleasure of sleeping, in order to attach to the Lord in communication.

Let's move now to the first point that is the effect of sin. We all are aware that sin creates a distance between God and us. Each one of us would like to live a life of holiness in the presence of God. This very first Sunday of Advent, Jesus Christ calls us to avoid all sins which take away our rationality. He called out drunkenness as an example. Think for a moment, when a person is drunk, he/she loses the gift of rationality. It is not only with drunkenness that a person loses the gift of rationality, but also with all sins such as pornography, pride, envy, etc. All sins take away our rationality. Therefore, on the very first Sunday of Advent, Jesus Christ is calling us to get over sins and use the gift of rationality to prepare the way of the Lord.

The third and final point of today's homily is that Jesus wants us to overcome worldly anxiety. Jesus is not talking about a medical anxiety here. The Greek word used here is *merimna,* which means "worry for this world." With the season of Christmas, you can see the shopping malls are being decorated, and digital advertising campaigns promote the buying of gifts. Most of us are worried about the new style in the market or what to buy or when to organize the Christmas parties. Indeed, Christmas is a season of receiving gifts, and giving gifts, and it's a season to come together to celebrate the joyful moments. However, it must not be the center of Advent to give gifts or to receive gifts. We must not forget that the reason for this season is Jesus Christ, Himself, who became flesh and lived among us. Therefore, it must be a time to prepare ourselves to receive Jesus while going to confession, actively participating in the liturgical celebrations and doing more acts of mercy towards our needy brothers and sisters.

May the powerful intercession of the Blessed Virgin Mary be our strength to stay awake and pray, in order to welcome the Messiah of the world!

## Reflect and Journal

# Second Sunday of Advent (B)

> Is 40:1-5, 9-11; Ps 85:9-14; 2 Pt 3:8-14 & Mk 1:1-8

## New Exodus + Humility = Promised Heaven

Dear sisters and brothers in Christ,

With the arrival of St. John the Baptist, we begin the second week of Advent. This week, I would like to journey with you to deepen our understanding of three points: wilderness, River Jordan and "mightier than I". Prior to the Gospel reflection, I would like to briefly highlight the importance of the character of John the Baptist and the Nativity of the Lord Jesus Christ.

As you may know, Holy Mother Church traditionally celebrates the birth of John the Baptist on June 24. Why? Think for a moment, the Annunciation to Mary, as tradition goes, took place in the month of

March, or more specifically, March 25. During the Annunciation to Mary, the Angel Gabriel also told Mary that her cousin Elizabeth was six months pregnant. In response to the angel's message, Mary went in haste to serve Elizabeth and remained there for three months, as the evangelist Luke recorded in the gospel (Lk 1:56). In that way, Mary was in the house of Zechariah and Elizabeth during the months of April, May and June; therefore, John the Baptist was born in the month of June. At the birth of John the Baptist, Mary was already three months pregnant; and from June to December are another six months. Six months after John the Baptist's birth, Jesus, the Savior of the World, was born in December.

Besides being a historical and liturgical point, there is a deeper theological meaning of the birth of St. John the Baptist in the month of June. Actually, I learned this from my grandfather who was a farmer, and later I learned it once again, in the academic circle, while reading a book of Joseph Ratzinger (Pope Benedict XVI), *"The Spirit of the Liturgy."*

If you pay attention, during the month of June, in its last days (Summer Solstice), the days get gradually shorter, shorter and shorter, until we reach the Winter Solstice, which is the shortest day of the year. And then, with Christmas - the birth of Jesus, which also comes towards the end of the month of December, the daylight begins to lengthen, lengthen and lengthen, until we go back to the Summer Solstice, which is in late June. What can you observe in this cosmic change, a movement of salvation? When darkness is prolonged in the world, John the Baptist is preaching and preparing the way of the Lord; and when the birth of Jesus takes place, this darkness loses its presence because the Light of Christ has entered this world. Consider an extract from the book of Joseph Ratzinger as a summary of relations between two miraculous births in the months of June and December and the cosmic change:

> ... the feast of the forerunner, St. John the Baptist, on June 24, at the time of the Summer Solstice. The link between the

> dates can now be seen as a liturgical and cosmic expression of the Baptist's words: "He [Christ] must increase, but I must decrease." (Jn 3:30). The birthday of St. John the Baptist takes place on the date when the days begin to shorten, just as the birthday of Christ takes place when they begin again to lengthen.
> Joseph Ratzinger,
> *The Spirit of the Liturgy*, 109

With this brief explanation about the character of John the Baptist, let's reflect to understand three points of today's Gospel.

We begin with the first point, which is the wilderness, where John the Baptist was preaching about the preparation. Just think for a moment, after their freedom from Egyptian slavery and miraculously crossing the Red Sea, the Israelites entered into the wilderness to prepare themselves to enter into the Promised Land. It was their preparation and faithfulness to the Lord that actually prepared them to enter into the Promised Land. In the same manner, Holy

Mother Church invites us to enter into the Holy Season of Advent in order to prepare ourselves to celebrate the Birth of Our Savior, Jesus Christ. To say briefly, as the wilderness experience of Exodus prepared the Israelites to enter into the Promised Land, so the Holy Season of Advent - the New Exodus - helps the community of believers to enter into the Promised Heaven. As the entry point into the Promised Land was the River Jordan, so too in the New Testament, the entry became the River Jordan. This is the second point of today's reflection.

John the Baptist starts baptizing the people in the River Jordan where the Old Exodus actually ended. Just consider the following reference:

> When the people set out from their tents to cross over the Jordan, the priests bearing the ark of the covenant were in front of the people. Now the Jordan overflows all its banks throughout the time of harvest. So when those who bore the ark had come to the Jordan and the feet of the priests

bearing the ark were dipped in the edge of the water, the waters flowing from above stood still, rising up in a single heap far off at Adam, the city that is beside Zarethan, while those flowing toward the Salt Sea of the Arabah, the Dead Sea, were wholly cut off. Then the people crossed over opposite Jericho. While all Israel were crossing over on dry ground, the priests who bore the ark of the covenant of the Lord stood firmly on dry ground in the middle of the Jordan, until the entire nation finished crossing over the Jordan.
Joshua 3:14-17

In that way, John the Baptist, the prophet of the New Exodus, actually started baptizing at the place where the Old Exodus ended. When Jesus received Baptism there, we can see that there was no longer water divided into two parts as happened in the Old Exodus, but in the New Exodus heaven was opened, which is the New Exodus for the community of believers.

We can only enter in the New Exodus with the attitude of humility, which is the third point of today's reflection. While belonging to the priestly class, seen by the people and appreciated by the community, John the Baptist still observed the virtue of humility. His head did not get big, but what we see is that he became humble. His humility showed that he was waiting for the Messiah. Therefore he confessed, "One mightier than I is coming after me."

Dear sisters and brothers, on this second Sunday of Advent we are invited by John the Baptist to join the New Exodus which was begun by Jesus Christ. Also, John the Baptist shows the way to enter into the New Exodus through humility, which is "the mother of all virtues" (St. John Eudes).

May the powerful intercession of the Blessed Virgin Mary be with us to journey in this New Exodus with humility, to encounter, embrace and serve Jesus.

# Reflect and Journal

# Third Sunday of Advent (A) Gaudete Sunday

> Isa 35:1-6,10; Ps 146;
> Jas 5:7-10 & Mt 11:2-11

## Arrival of the Holy One of Israel Among Us!

Dear sisters and brothers in Christ,

The Gospel passage for this Sunday once again invites us to walk with John the Baptist to encounter Jesus Christ. Indeed, the purpose and meaning of Advent is to encounter Jesus Christ. As Pope St. Paul VI said, "We consider Christmas as the encounter, the great encounter, the historical encounter, the decisive encounter, between God and mankind . . ."

Last week, which was the second week of Advent, we saw that John the Baptist went to the River Jordan, the place where the "Old Exodus" ended and the Israelites entered the

Promised Land. His action of giving a baptism of repentance in that place was a sign of preparation to begin the "New Exodus," which our Lord Jesus started through His own baptism, thereby opening heaven for us. And so, all the baptized are invited to no longer look for the Promised Land, but to get ready for the Promised Heaven where John the Baptist will join us!

To unlock the mystery of the third Sunday of Advent, let's begin with the question of John the Baptist, "Are you the one who is to come, or should we look for another?" Take a closer look at the question of John the Baptist, which says "Are you the one who is to come . . ." He did not say, "Are you the Messiah . . ." In Hebrew traditions, "one who is to come . . ." was an expression used for the God of Israel, the Holy one of Israel. In simple words, John the Baptist asked Jesus, "Are you the LORD of Israel?"

To reveal His Divinity in the Gospels, Jesus always gave indirect references, as we can see in today's Gospel. In response to John the Baptist's question, Jesus revealed His Divinity through his ministry:

> ... the blind regain their sight,
> the lame walk,
> lepers are cleansed,
> the deaf hear,
> the dead are raised,
> and the poor have the good news proclaimed to them.

In short, Jesus not only referred to His ministry, but He told John the Baptist to read the prophetic traditions, particularly to read from the prophet Isaiah and the prophet Elisha, where Jesus' Divinity, the LORD of Israel, had been revealed.

Together, let's see the first reference from today's first reading:

> *Be strong, fear not! Here is your God ... [God] comes to save you. Th en will the eyes of the blind be opened, the ears of the deaf be cleared; then will the lame leap like a stag, then the tongue of the mute will sing.*
> Isaiah 35:1-6 [emphasis added]

The second reference comes from the Second Book of Kings, where the prophet Elisha, through the power of the Holy One of Israel, healed the leper Naaman. As you can read in the story, the king of Aram wrote a letter to the king of Israel, instructing him to heal Naaman from his leprosy. As soon as the king of Israel received the letter from the king of Aram, he tore his robes and said, "Am I God, to give death or life, that this man sends words to me to cure of his leprosy?" (2 Kings 5:7). After his own healing of leprosy, Naaman, a non-believer, confessed, "Now I know that there is no God in all the earth except in Israel" (2 Kings 5:15). In other words, only the LORD of Israel can heal leprosy!!!

So in response to the question of John the Baptist regarding "Are you the one...," Jesus once again quoted from the prophetic traditions and said, "Lepers are cleansed." In fact, there is another saying that the HOLY ONE OF ISRAEL had already arrived. John the Evangelist wonderfully said it in the Gospel:

> The Word became flesh and lived among us, and we have seen his glory, the glory as of a father's only son, full of grace and truth.
> John 1:14

Dear sisters and brothers, let's not forget that Christmas is the arrival of the HOLY ONE OF ISRAEL among us. Let's not allow our Christmas to only become a social event or another holiday, but in the depth of our hearts, let's listen to the words of Jesus, who lives among us in the poor, the sick, the homeless and the stranger. As we are preparing ourselves to celebrate Christmas, let's encounter Jesus Christ in the poor, the needy, the homeless and the sick, as we sing in the famous Christian song:

> Whatsoever you do to the least of my people
> That you do unto me.
> When I was hungry, you gave me to eat;
> When I was thirsty you gave me to drink.
> Now enter into the home of my Father.

May Mary, the mother of Jesus and our mother, intercede for us so that we may have an encounter with the Holy One of Israel who has come among us to heal the sick, cleanse the lepers, give sight to the blind, grant hearing to the mute and raise the dead.

# Reflect and Journal

# Third Sunday of Advent (B)
## *Gaudete Sunday*

Is 61:1-2A, 10-11; Lk 1:46-50, 53-54;
1 Thes 5:16-24 & Jn 1:6-8, 19-28

**Rejoice and Pray without Ceasing**

Dear sisters and brothers in Christ,

Let's rejoice and celebrate the third Sunday of the Holy Season of Advent, known as *Gaudete* Sunday. The Latin word *Gaudete* stands for "rejoice." Therefore, you can see that on this Sunday the priest wears a rose chasuble, and a rose candle on the Advent wreath is lighted (rose, not pink!!!). Consequently, *Gaudete* Sunday is also known as "Rose Sunday." This week, what I propose is to journey together to understand the deeper meaning of the word "rejoice" (χαίρω - *charió*) and the expression used by St. Paul, "pray without ceasing."

First and foremost, in the Sacred Scripture, "rejoice" can be found just under 200 times, and it stands as a command. It is one of those commands in the Sacred Scripture which is frequently repeated as a reminder to rejoice in the Lord. In reality, the word "rejoice" speaks for itself, as:

R stands for **REPENT**
E stands for **EMBRACE**
J stands for **JOY** to be
O stands for **ONE**
I stands for **IN**
C stands for **CHRIST**
E stands for **ETERNALLY**

Every time the command of "rejoice" comes up in the Sacred Scripture, it actually stands with an invitation of repentance. This act of a believer, which is to repent from one's sinful way, actually brings great joy in heaven, as Jesus said, "I tell you, there will be more joy in heaven over one sinner who repents than over ninety-nine righteous persons who need no repentance" (Luke 15:7). Therefore, Holy Mother Church in this holy Season of Advent encourages the community of believers to repent from their sins to embrace Christ.

The second letter in "rejoice" is "E," which stands for "embrace." Once we repent from our sinful deeds, we are on the way to embracing the joy of the Heavenly Father.

The third letter of "rejoice" is "J," which stands for "joy." After we repent and get ready to embrace our salvation, we actually go through inner joy. This feeling of inner joy comes through the very act of repentance, in which a person feels a gentle embrace of the Heavenly Father. Henri J. Nouwen expresses this joy as "an experience of knowing that you are unconditionally loved" (from his book, *Here and Now: Living in the Spirit*). This feeling of unconditional love helps a person to be one in Christ eternally, as "O" stands for "one," "I" for "in," "C" for "Christ," and "E" stands for "eternally." Therefore always rejoice, that is, "Repent to Embrace the Joy of being One in Christ Eternally."

The second point of today's reflection is to pray without ceasing. Now St. Paul not only in Thessalonians but throughout several of his letters (Romans 1:9 & 2 Timothy 1:3) emphasizes the practice of praying without ceasing. First and foremost, St. Paul did not write about this pious practice of praying without ceasing as an expression, but he wanted to emphasize the importance of praying. Indeed, praying is a dialogue, and to pray without ceasing is an action of getting into a dialogue with God, because unceasing prayer is to think, speak and live in the presence of God. This act of praying without ceasing should be an act of *uncensored* prayer, as found in the Holy Book of the Psalms:

> Listen to my words, O LORD; attend to my sighing. *Listen to the sound of my cry*, my King and my God, for to you I pray.
> Psalm 5:1-2 (emphasis added)

> My God, my God, why have you forsaken me? Why are you so far from helping me, from the words of groaning? *O my God, I cry by day, but you do not answer; and by night,*

> *but find no rest.*
> Psalm 22:1-2 (emphasis added)

> *I cry aloud to God, aloud to God, that he may hear me.* On the day of my trouble I seek the Lord; in the night my hand is stretched out without wearying; my soul refuses to be comforted.
> Psalm 77:1-2 (emphasis added)

Dear sisters and brothers, it is our acts of rejoicing, that is, "Repent to Embrace the Joy of being One in Christ Eternally" and praying without ceasing that actually help us to witness the miraculous arrival of Jesus Christ in our world. Therefore, let's in turn carry out the lighting of the rose candle to witness the Birth of Jesus Christ in our hearts, homes and society.

May the powerful intercession of the Blessed Virgin Mary be our strength to carry the Light of Christ to rejoice and pray without ceasing.

## Reflect and Journal

# Fourth Sunday of Advent (A)

> Is 7:10-14; Ps 24;
> Rom 1:1-7 and Mt 1:18-24

## Through a Virgin, the Saviour Has Entered into the World

Dear sisters and brothers in Christ,

On this Fourth Sunday of Advent, we have the passage from the Gospel of Matthew known as "the Annunciation to St. Joseph." The annunciation to St. Joseph invites us to focus on three points: 1. a virgin bears a son; 2. the words that St. Joseph "had no marital relations with her until she had given birth to a son" (Matthew 1:25); and 3. the character of St. Joseph, whose actions speak louder than words. As you can see, we have a lot to unlock with regard to the Gospel today. Therefore, let's begin with Mary as a virgin, or as Catholics expressly say through faith, Mary as "ever-virgin."

One of the common questions which I'm often asked by both non-Catholics and Catholics alike, and I believe that most of you have also faced this question at least once in your life, is how can Mary be "ever-virgin," when she already gave birth to a child? As a cradle Catholic, I also had some difficulty understanding this, which led me to become anti-Marian quite a while back. During my pastoral and academic ministry, I have also encountered Catholics who accept Mary as a holy woman, but when it comes to her virginity, they are not comfortable or not equipped well enough to express the faith and plan of God. Often, I would hear them say, "We don't care if Mary is a virgin or not." But I do care, the Church cares, and our forefathers in faith cared!!! This i s b ecause Mary's virginity, or calling her "ever-virgin," is not only a physical condition, but rather, it is way beyond that.

When the angel brought the good news to St. Jospeh, the angel quoted from the prophetic traditions and said, "Behold, the virgin shall conceive and bear a son." While reading the account of the annunciation to Mary from the Gospel of Luke, we come to know that the angel Gabriel was sent to Nazareth to a virgin whose name was Mary (Luke 1:26). Indeed, Mary herself confessed that she is a virgin when she said, "How can this be, *since I am a virgin*?" (Luke 1:34 - emphasis added)

Biblically speaking, when the evangelists Matthew and Luke called Mary the virgin mother, they were actually pointing towards the New Creation which was about to take place through the conception of Jesus in the womb of Mary. First and foremost, who was the first virgin female character in the Holy Bible? It was "Woman," the helper of Adam. She was placed in the Garden of Eden to be with Adam. She was a virgin and full of grace because "Woman" had not committed any sin yet; in other words, she was sinless, and so we can conclude here that in the Old Creation, "Woman," the helper of Adam, was a virgin, and she was full of grace and sinless! As the Book of Genesis tells us, God walked and talked everyday with Adam and

"Woman," who was a virgin, full of grace and sinless. But she lost her state of virginity (that is, being full of grace) when she fell into sin. As a result, she was no longer a virgin, she was no longer full of grace, and she was no longer sinless. Therefore, her name was changed from "Woman" to Eve. It is through the fall of a virgin that sin entered into the world.

To restore what was lost in the Old Creation by a virgin, full of grace, both evangelists, Matthew and Luke, gave the narratives of the birth of Jesus with both significantly mentioning a virgin, full of grace. In the Old Creation, sin entered the world through a virgin, and so in the New Creation, it is also through a virgin, full of grace, that salvation entered into the world. And so, when Sacred Scripture calls Mary a virgin, the church teaches the community of believers that Mary is "ever-virgin," and when we confess that Mary is a virgin, we are actually confessing that through the womb of Mary, salvation entered into our world.

Now, we move on to our second point, and that is, St. Joseph "had no marital relations with her until she had given birth to a son" (Matthew 1:25). Most of us understand this verse as St. Joseph having marital relations with Mary after the birth of Jesus because the verse says, "no marital relations with [Mary] UNTIL she had given birth to a son." Please note that the Biblical meaning of UNTIL is different. Let's together look at this tricky word, UNTIL, which often creates much confusion.

> . . . Michal the daughter of Saul had no child *to the day of or [until] her death*
> 2 Samuel 6:23 (emphasis added)

Does this mean that she had children after she died? Let's take another passage:

> [Paul said], *Until I arrive*, give attention to the public reading of scripture, to exhorting, to teaching.
> 1 Timothy 4:13 (emphasis added)

Does this mean that Timothy should stop teaching after Paul comes?

> [Paul wrote] For he [Christ] must reign *until* he has put all his enemies under his feet.
> 1 Corinthians 15:25 (emphasis added)

Does this mean Christ's reign will end when his enemies are under his feet?

As we can observe, UNTIL does not mean "for some time," but rather, it stands for "forever." Therefore, when Matthew says, "no marital relations until," it stands for "no relations before the birth and after the birth of Jesus."

Now we move on to the third and final point of today's Gospel, and that is, "[Joseph] did as the angel of the Lord had commanded him." This means that he listened carefully and changed the plan in his life, which was originally to quietly leave Mary and not to accept Jesus as his child. Instead, when he heard the voice of God through the angel, he accepted Mary as she was and brought her into his home. Joseph did not question the plan of God. He simply brought Mary into his home, because he understood that Mary was carrying in her womb Jesus, the Savior of the world. And so, let's not forget that we are all called to be like Joseph - to carry Mary, a virgin, full of grace and sinless, in our minds, hearts and homes, because where Mary is, there Jesus is also; and where Jesus is, there Mary is also. In our Eudist traditions, we say, "to Jesus through Mary."

May Mary, the mother of Jesus and our mother, a virgin, full of grace and sinless, intercede for us, so that we may accept Jesus, the Savior of the world, as she did during her entire earthly life.

# Reflect and Journal

# Fourth Sunday of Advent (B)

> 2 Sm 7:1-5, 8b-12, 14a 16; Ps 89:2-5, 27, 29;
> Rom 16:25-27 & Lk 1:26-38

## New Davidic Kingdom

Dear sisters and brothers in Christ,

On the Fourth Sunday of Advent (B), the Gospel passage, which is taken from the Gospel of Luke, is known as the "Annunciation to Mary." Indeed, this passage is so rich in itself that in just 0.37 seconds, Google shows 8,180,000 book results. Besides a Google book search, if you look for Annunciation to Mary in Christian art, in just 0.35 seconds, you will find 12,000,000 results. In addition to books, paintings, and numerous songs, religious devotions took shape through the inspiration of the Annunciation to Mary. In fact, St. John Eudes, while establishing the Congregation of Jesus & Mary (Eudist Fathers), found his spiritual inspiration in this Gospel passage as the foundation for the Congregation of Jesus & Mary, which he later expressed in his letter, "Missionaries of Mercy."

Since we can see that there is a lot going on in today's Gospel – the Annunciation to Mary – what I would actually like to propose is that we walk together to deepen our understanding about the characters of St. Joseph and the Blessed Virgin Mary. What a time to make a change, Fr. Azam! You just said that this Gospel passage is on the Annunciation to Mary, but you want to focus on St. Joseph also? Why!?!?

As I always preach and teach, we have to revisit our theology to deepen our understanding of the Sacred Scripture. The Annunciation to Mary is not only a call to the Blessed Virgin Mary to be the Mother of the Messiah, but it is actually the promise of establishing the Davidic Kingdom, where St. Joseph stands as a key character and Mary as the Queen Mother. So actually what we are going to do today is focus on three things: St. Joseph, a key character of the Davidic Kingdom; Mary, the Queen Mother in the

Davidic Kingdom; and of course, Jesus, the center of all things. Prior to unlocking the mystery of the Davidic Kingdom in the Annunciation to Mary, let's quickly see in the Gospel text where the Kingdom of David is mentioned:

> The angel Gabriel was sent ... to a virgin betrothed to a man named *Joseph, of the house of David,* and the virgin's name was Mary.

> [Angel Gabriel said] ... the Lord God will give him *the throne of David his father* ... and of *his kingdom there will be no end.*

In both texts, three things are significant - Joseph, the throne of David, and no end of the kingdom. In this way, what we observe is that the Annunciation is not only a call to the Blessed Mary to be the Mother of the Messiah, but it is an announcement of the establishment of the Davidic Kingdom. The kingdom built by David was an earthly, powerful kingdom, but what we see in the Old Testament is that it did not last forever. In reality, the kingdom of Israel first was divided into parts known as the Southern Kingdom or the Kingdom of Judah and the Northern Kingdom or the Kingdom of Israel. Not only that, Israel as a nation also went into slavery. In brief, the kingdom of David was looking for a new heir who could re-establish the kingdom.

In that case, Jesus, the Divine Son of God born of the Blessed Virgin Mary, actually finds his lineage through St. Joseph who was from the house of David. In the Annunciation to Mary, through the Birth of Jesus, a promise was made that there would be no end to Jesus' Kingdom. There is no doubt that the kingdom built by David went through a crisis and slavery, but the Kingdom of Jesus, established through His Birth, in fact will overcome the slavery of sin and will never again go into slavery.

While keeping this in mind, we move to the second point of today's reflection to ask:

"What is the significance of Mary being the Queen Mother in the Kingdom of Jesus!?!?"

In the Israelite Kingdom, a wife of a king was not chosen as a queen or, in other words, there was no First Lady, because the king had a huge number of wives:

> [Solomon] among his wives were *seven hundred princesses and three hundred concubines* . . .
> 1 Kings 11:3 (emphasis added)

Among a huge number of wives, I am sure the king did not want any trouble from choosing a wife as his First Lady. Also, the wives were not allowed in the court. So who was the queen in the Kingdom of Israel? The mother of the king was the queen, and she was addressed as Queen Mother. She was the only woman who had free access to the court of the king. She could freely talk to the king in the presence of his members, and the king never refused his mother. Let's review the Bible passage:

> He said, "Please ask King Solomon—*he will not refuse you* . . . Bathsheba said, "Very well; I will speak to the king on your behalf."
> 1 Kings 2:17 (emphasis added)

Look at the entrance of the Queen Mother into the court and the king's attitude towards her:

> So Bathsheba went to King Solomon . . . The king *rose* to meet her and *bowed down* to her; then he sat on his throne, and *had a throne* brought for the king's mother, and *she sat on his right.*
> 1 Kings 2:19 (emphasis added)

The king had absolute power in his kingdom and did not need to leave his throne in order to welcome someone. But we can see that when his mother came in, he rose; he bowed down and gave her a place at his right hand, which is a symbol of power and respect.

The Queen Mother went into the court not for herself, but she brought the request:

> She said, "I have one small request to make of you; *do not refuse* me."
> 1 Kings 2:20 (emphasis added)

The Queen Mother always intercedes for others, and in reply, this is what the king does:

> The king said to her, "Make your request, my mother; *for I will not refuse you.*"
> 1 Kings 2:21 (emphasis added)

Now, when we call Jesus our King, and he who is greater than Solomon (Mt 12:42), we are acknowledging Mary as our Queen Mother. Whenever we turn towards Mary and seek her intercession, she always brings us to Jesus, and the Sacred Scriptures tell us that Jesus never refused His mother. We Catholics are so blessed to have the Queen Mother who is always interceding for us. That is why we should take a moment of silence to seek the intercession of Mary while praying in our hearts for whatever we need from Jesus.

Dear sisters and brothers in Christ, the Fourth Sunday of Advent (B) is a reminder for us that Jesus is establishing the New Davidic Kingdom where St. Joseph and the Blessed Virgin Mary are leading us to follow Jesus Christ as our Savior.

May the powerful intercession of the Blessed Mother strengthen us to embrace the Kingdom of Jesus through the Birth of her only Son, Jesus Christ.

# Reflect and Journal

# Fourth Sunday of Advent (C)

> Mi 5:1-4a; Ps 80:2-3, 15-16, 18-19;
> Heb 10:5-10 & Lk 1:39-45

## The Twofold Gifts of Mary's Greeting

Dear sisters and brothers in Christ,

The Fourth Sunday of Advent (C) invites us to journey together with Blessed Mary to bring the Good News to Elizabeth, who is ashamed of her old age pregnancy. The Gospel passage is known as the "visitation to Elizabeth" (Lk 1:39-45). Mary and Elizabeth were cousins, and when Mary came to know about Elizabeth's pregnancy through the mouth of the Angel Gabriel, she went in haste to serve her cousin Elizabeth.

Before we begin our journey to understand today's Gospel passage, let me give you a panoramic view of Advent Season. Advent is a penitential season in which the community of believers is encouraged to repent in order to prepare themselves to welcome the birth of Jesus Christ among themselves. The First Sunday of Advent was an invitation to repent and get ready to enter the Kingdom of God. On the second and third Sundays of Advent, we saw the penitential ministry and moral teachings of John the Baptist. Once again, the running theme was to repent and to share your blessings with all those who are in need. The fourth Sunday of Advent highlights the character of Mary, who went in haste to serve Elizabeth while carrying Jesus Christ, the Savior of the world, in her womb.

On the Fourth Sunday of Advent, the Gospel passage, the "visitation to Elizabeth" (Lk 1:39-45), is covered in several layers through which we can understand the dialogue between the two women who were chosen unexpectedly to serve in the plan of God. To unpack the Gospel passage & deepen our understanding, I would like to journey with you while reflecting together on three points: 1. Mary went in haste; 2. the twofold gift of Mary's greeting to Elizabeth and 3. the twofold beatitudes of Elizabeth for Mary. Let's begin with the immediate action of Mary after the Annunciation, that *"[she] went with haste."*

"Mary went with haste into the hill country" is an immediate action of Mary after hearing the Good News from the Angel Gabriel, where Angel Gabriel told Mary, *"The Holy Spirit will come upon you, and the power of the Most High will overshadow you;* therefore the child to be born will be holy; he will be called Son of God" (Lk 1:35-36, emphasis added). Through this action of Mary that "[*she*] went in haste," the Evangelist Luke wants to emphasize that Mary is not only a listener of the Word, but she acted upon on it.

In this action of Mary, the Evangelist Luke gives us another perspective on Mary's character as she went from north in Galilee to south into the hill country. To briefly comment about the geography of Israel, Nazareth is in Galilee, which is in the north of Israel. The north of Israel has green fields, pastures and farmland. It is very rich and lush. On the other hand, the south of Israel, "the hill country of Judah," is hilly and rocky. It's difficult to walk there, and you get easily tired. After the Annunciation, Mary left her comfort-zone to help her cousin Elizabeth, who lived in the hill country. In a way, the Evangelist Luke is telling us that Mary reaches out to all those who are in need of Jesus Christ, AMEN!

After a long journey of travelling from north to south, Mary entered the house of her cousin Elizabeth and greeted her. This greeting of Mary brought twofold gifts: first, after hearing the greeting of Mary, Elizabeth experienced that the baby, "John the Baptist," leapt in her womb. Elizabeth, who was living in shame and hiding from the world because of her old age pregnancy, must have been going through stress and anxiety. But as Mary greeted her, not only Elizabeth, but even the unborn baby, "John the Baptist," leapt in her womb to acknowledge that she was bringing the Good News. I had always thought that the baby leapt in his mother's womb in the presence of Jesus, who was in the womb of His mother. However, it was only this year that I noticed that the baby leapt in his mother's womb with the greeting of Mary.

Second, Mary's greeting also brought the gift of the Holy Spirit. When Elizabeth heard the greeting of Mary, not only did the baby leap in his mother's womb, but Elizabeth was also filled with the Holy Spirit. "Elizabeth heard the greeting of Mary . . . Elizabeth was filled the Holy Spirit . . . ." In a way, Mary, who was carrying the Savior of the world in her womb when she greeted Elizabeth, who was living in shame and anxiety, actually caused Elizabeth to not only experience the Good News of Jesus Christ, who was in the womb of His mother, but also to be filled with the Holy Spirit.

After experiencing the twofold gifts with the greeting of Mary, Elizabeth, who was filled with the Holy Spirit, also gave twofold beatitudes: "Blessed are you *among women* and blessed is the *fruit of your womb.*" The first beatitude was for Mary who had been chosen among the women, and the second beatitude was a confession that what was in the womb of Mary is BLESSED, He is the Holy One, and He is the Savior of the World. We can see this confession of Elizabeth in the following statement, "why has this happened to me, that the mother of *my Lord* comes to me?"

May the powerful intercession of the Blessed Virgin Mary help us to embrace the Good News of Jesus Christ who is the Savior of the world.

# Reflect and Journal

# The Solemnity of the Nativity of the Lord (Christmas) - (B)

Is 9:1-6; Ps 96:1-3, 11-13; Ti 2:11-14 & Lk 2:1-14

## Bethlehem + Manger = Jesus, the Divine Bread

Dear sisters and brothers in Christ,

On the Solemnity of the Birth of Jesus Christ, our Savior, once again we are being invited by Holy Mother Church to go together to Bethlehem to adore Jesus Christ, who left His heavenly throne to be laid in a manger, and a loud message from the angels said, "do not be afraid." The English word, Christmas, is actually a combination of two words - *Khrīstos* (Χριστός), which in Greek stands for Christ or anointed one, and *Missa* which in Latin stands for worship. Putting these words together actually gives birth to an English word - **CHRISTMAS** - which means "Christ's worship" or "let's go to adore the

Christ." Therefore, join me in praising the Lord as we travel on the road to Bethlehem singing:

> O come, all ye faithful, joyful and triumphant
> O come ye, O come ye to Bethlehem
> Come and behold Him, born the King of Angels
>
> O come, let us adore Him
> O come, let us adore Him
> O come, let us adore Him
> Christ the Lord

We have come to adore the Christ - AMEN! We have come to worship the Christ - AMEN! And we have come to receive the Christ - AMEN! The Gospel passage about the Nativity of the Lord is taken from the Gospel of Luke. To unlock the mystery of the Gospel passage, let's journey together to explore only two things: Bethlehem and the manger.

The Hebrew word בית לחם (Bethlehem), is a mixture of two words. The first Hebrew word, בית (*beth*), stands for house, and the second word, לחם (*laham*) stands for bread. So putting together these two words we get the word - Bethlehem - which means "the House of Bread." Now think for a moment that the Birth of Jesus Christ in the House of Bread was not an accident, but it was a clear message to humanity that Jesus Christ had arrived in the House of Bread, but not as simple bread, but as Divine Bread. Where, actually was this Divine Bread placed!?!? In a manger!!! Just on a lighter note, Jesus was not born in a manger, He was actually placed in a manger. With this in mind, we move to a second and final point, the manger.

Often we overlook the manger, but for St. Luke, the manger was so important that he mentioned it three times in the Nativity episode (Lk 2:7, 12, 16). In fact, the manger was a sign of the Messiah. Consider the three Gospel passages:

> [Mary] gave birth to her first born son and wrapped him in bands of cloth, and *laid him in a manger*, because there was no place for them in the inn.
> Luke 2:7 [emphasis added]

> [The Angel told the shepherds] "This will be a sign for you: *you will find a child wrapped in bands of cloth and lying in a manger.*" Luke 2:12 [emphasis added]

> So [the shepherds] went with haste and found Mary and Joseph, and *the child lying in the manger.*
> Luke 2:16 [emphasis added]

What actually was the manger? First and foremost, what we see today as a manger, made of good wood and covered with fancy clothes and decorations, actually has nothing to do with the Biblical manger. A manger was a feeding trough which was made out of stone. It was the place where animals went and put their (sometimes dirty) mouths inside to eat their meals.

Now, think for a moment, Jesus was born in Bethlehem - the House of Bread, and was laid in the manger. Indeed, this was a visible message that He became the food for all . . . for the righteous as well as for sinners. Everyone, I mean it, **EVERYONE!!!** Therefore, the righteous and the sinners, metaphorically speaking, can put their mouths into the manger to receive the Christ - the Divine Bread from heaven. This is what Jesus did at the Last Supper while He offered His Body and Blood to His disciples and said, "take all of you and eat" and "take all of you and drink" (Mark 14:22-24). Jesus did not say, "Take all of you, except you, Judas Iscariot!" Jesus could have simply said that, since Judas was about to betray Him. But Jesus allowed Judas to receive His Body and Blood - Amen! And today, Jesus allows each one of us to receive in a worthy manner the Body and Blood of the one who was born in Bethlehem and laid in a manger. Therefore, do not be afraid to approach Jesus, who was laid in a manger, as our food for eternity. Therefore, let's once again meet Jesus on the road to Bethlehem and sing together:

> O come, all ye faithful, joyful and triumphant
> O come ye, O come ye to Bethlehem
> Come and behold Him, born the King of Angels
>
> O come, let us adore Him
> O come, let us adore Him
> O come, let us adore Him
> Christ the Lord

Let's turn towards the Blessed Virgin Mary, who offered her only Son to be the food of salvation, to intercede for us so that we may approach the manger, the Altar of the Lord, to receive the Body and Blood of Jesus Christ on our journey to heaven.

# Reflect and Journal

# Feast of the Holy Family of Jesus, Mary and Joseph (B)

> Sir 3:2-6, 12-14; Ps 128:1-5;
> Col 3:12-21 & Lk 2:22-40

## Obedience + Love = Salvation - Jesus Christ

Dear sisters and brothers in Christ,

As we are continuing to celebrate the festivities of the Birth of Our Blessed Lord, once again we are being invited by Holy Mother Church to ponder the basic unit of society, that is, "family," in order to draw from it holiness and receive the gift of salvation, while imitating the example of the Holy Family. This week, I would like to journey with you to explore three questions:
1. What causes a holy family to be holy?
2. What should be the law of the family?

3. What is the gift of being obedient to the Law of the Lord and practicing it every day in the family?

To unpack the mystery of these questions let's begin with a basic one, "What makes a Holy Family to be holy?" Actually, it is obedience to the Law of the Lord, as reflected in the Gospel passage (Lk 2:22-40):

> When the days were completed for their purification *according to the Law of Moses,* they [Joseph and Mary] took him [Jesus] up to Jerusalem to present him to the Lord . . . to offer the sacrifice of a pair of turtledoves or two young pigeons *in accordance with the dictates in the law of the Lord.*
> Luke 2:22-40 [emphasis added]

Just think for a moment, Joseph and Mary did not only receive the Angel Gabriel and the divine messages through the Angel. They also saw the hand of the LORD in the miraculous Birth of Jesus, with Mary conceiving Jesus while she was a Virgin; a sign with Elizabeth getting pregnant in her old age; the shepherds brought the angelic message to Joseph and Mary; and the Magi visiting the baby Jesus and finding Him with Mary.

There were other events which took place during the Nativity of the Lord, and each event was a revelation to the parents of Jesus, that He was the Messiah; but still, Joseph and Mary were obedient to the Law of the LORD. They could have simply said that they did not need any Law because they had the Messiah! On the contrary, Joseph and Mary brought Jesus to the Temple and offered the sacrifice for their only Child, as per the Law of Moses given by the Lord. So what we can say is that the gift of holiness in the family comes from keeping the Law of the Lord in the family.

Now we can ask a second question, "What should be the law of the family?" Each family has certain laws and traditions. I remember well that in my family, on Christmas morning, my grandfather would pray the Psalms as an act of Thanksgiving to the Lord. I think there is also a universal unwritten mother's law in the family that says, "If you don't finish your meal, you won't get your ice cream or dessert."

So what should be the law of the family? I believe the law of each family or community should be "love," as St. John Eudes says that "the law of all laws is charity [love]." St. Paul gives a wonderful description of love, which I believe helps not only families but communities to receive the gift of holiness. He says:

> Love is *patient*; love is *kind*; love is
> *not envious* or *boastful* or *arrogant* or *rude*.
> It *does not insist on its own way*; it is *not
> irritable*; it keeps *no record of wrongs*; it
> *does not rejoice in wrongdoing* but rejoices
> in the *truth*. It *bears* all things, *believes* all
> things, *hopes* all things, and *endures* all
> things. Love never ends.
> 1 Corinthians 13:4-8 [emphasis added]

There are many moments in the family when we lose our patience in a situation and we say unkind words. Sometimes we act rudely or arrogantly when forgiving family members. I invite each one of you to take this Pauline passage as a foundation for the family to receive the gift of holiness. What I also like in this passage is actually the advice of St. Paul that "love **bears** all things, **believes** all things, **hopes** all things, **endures** all things." These should be the four pillars of each family, that is, "bear, believe, hope and endure." Therefore, let's never lose love in the family, especially in moments of confusion, fights or disappointments.

While keeping love in our minds, hearts and souls, let's turn towards the last and final question of today's reflection, which is "What would be the result of keeping the law in the family?"

As I said earlier, obedience to the Law of the LORD actually leads each family to prepare itself to receive the gift of holiness and prepares family members to love each other. Now, as a result of obedience to the Law of the LORD and observing in the family the law of laws, which is love, we are led to the gift of salvation which comes only from

JESUS CHRIST. Simeon, who was led by the Holy Spirit in the Temple, held Jesus in his arms and confessed ". . . Now [Lord] . . . my eyes have seen your salvation."

Dear sisters and brothers in Christ, think for a moment that Joseph and Mary, under obedience to the Law of the LORD, while carrying Jesus among them and holding Jesus with love, even with all their difficulties, disappointments and challenges, they still held Jesus among themselves, and as a result, they encountered their gift of salvation.

We are invited by Holy Mother Church to imitate Joseph and Mary, that is, to carry Jesus while observing the Law of the Lord and to hold Jesus while loving our family members (biological and spiritual), in order to join Simeon in confessing that "Now [Lord] . . . my eyes have seen your salvation."

May the intercessions of the Blessed Virgin Mary and St. Joseph be our strength to obey the Law of the Lord and practice the law of love in our families, in order to receive Jesus Christ in our families as the gift of salvation.

## Reflect and Journal

# January 1
# Solemnity of the Blessed Virgin Mary, the Mother of God (A)

> Num 6:22-27; Ps 67:2-3, 5-6, 8;
> Gal 4:4-7 & Lk 2:16-21

## To Jesus Through Mary!

Dear sisters and brothers in Christ,

As we are celebrating the Solemnity of the Blessed Virgin Mary, the Mother of God, also known as Θεοτόκος (*Theotokos* "God-bearer" or "birth-giver to God"), the Church encourages us to look at Jesus, the Savior of the world born in Bethlehem, through the eyes of Mary. According to Jewish tradition, after the birth of a baby boy, a ceremony of circumcision was performed and the child's name was given on the eighth day. What name did Joseph and Mary give to their first and only child?... JESUS!!!

In today's readings, there is the gradual progress of a blessing taking place, as we see Moses giving the traditional priestly blessing (Num 6:22-27). The Psalmist calls this blessing the "blessing of mercy" (Ps 67:2-3), and for Paul, this "blessing of mercy" took flesh while "born of a woman" and "born under the law" (Gal 4:4). With this "blessing of mercy" came the fulfillment of the law, and the Savior was born of Mary. He was kept in a manger, and the shepherds came to adore Him in accordance with the instructions of an angel (Lk 2:16-21). To understand the relationship between the shepherds' visit to the child Jesus in the manger and the solemnity of Mary, the *Theotokos*, the Gospel passage invites us to ponder one point only, and that is, the shepherds found Mary with the infant Jesus who was laid in a manger.

Often I have preached, as well as taught, that the Marian solemnities or feasts are not about Mary, the Mother of Jesus; but rather, they highlight the divinity of Jesus, who was formed in the womb of Mary through the power of the Holy Spirit, who lived in the womb of Mary (Lk 1:26-38), and who later lived among us (Jn 1:14). To fully unlock the mystery of today's solemnity and to understand the Biblical truth and the profession of our forefathers in faith, let's briefly look at the history of this solemnity.

Arius (256 - 336 AD), who was a presbyter from Alexandria, Egypt, denied the Divinity of Jesus. From him, Arianism was born. According to him, Jesus was "created," and therefore, he is not from Eternity. However, the Church defended the Biblical truth and proclaimed at the Council of Nicaea (325 AD) that Jesus is from Eternity, as we say:

> I believe in one Lord Jesus Christ, the Only Begotten Son of God . . . God from God, Light from Light, true God from true God, begotten, not made, consubstantial with the Father; through him all things were made. For us men and for our salvation he came down from heaven, and by the Holy Spirit

was incarnate of the Virgin Mary, and became man.

Two other heresies of that time were called Docetism and Apollinarianism. Both heresies took place as a reaction to Arianism. They believed in the Divinity of Jesus, in contrast to Arianism, but both Docetism and Apollinarianism denied the humanity of Jesus.

According to Apollinarianism, the human mind forms all evil and deceit; therefore, Jesus didn't have a human mind. On the other hand, Docetism believed that the human body was entrapped in worldly evils like hatred, lust, bloodshed, gluttony and the like; and therefore, Jesus wasn't human. According to this heresy, Jesus' humanity was merely an appearance and not reality.

So the Council of Constantinople (381 AD) stood against these two heresies to proclaim the Biblical truth and confessed that Jesus is fully Divine and fully human because "the Word became flesh and lived among us" (John 1:14). And Mary carried Him in her womb as Elizabeth professed when the Holy Spirit came upon her, "Why has this happened to me, that the mother of my Lord (κύριος [Kyrios] - Lord, Savior) comes to me?" (Luke 1:43).

Nestorius, who was the Patriarch (Archbishop) of Constantinople, denied calling Mary *Theotokos* (God-bearer). For him, Mary was Χριστοτόκος (*Christotokos* - Christ-bearer), which means, Mary was the mother of the human Jesus. In other words, she was not the mother of the Divine Jesus. In brief, he saw the Divinity and the humanity of Jesus Christ as contradictory natures. The Council of Ephesus (431 AD) defended the Biblical truth that Jesus Christ was fully Divine and fully human. Therefore, Mary is the Mother of Jesus Christ who is fully Divine and fully human, as we can see in the Gospel of John:

> In the beginning was the Word, and the Word was with God, and the Word was God. He was in the beginning with God. All things came into being through him, and without him not one thing came

> into being. What has come into being in him was life, and the life was the light of all people ... And the Word became flesh and lived among us, and we have seen his glory, the glory as of a father's only son, full of grace and truth.
> (John 1:1-4 & 14)

To fully understand the passage, let's replace "Word" and "he" with the name of Jesus:

> In the beginning was [Jesus], and [Jesus] was with God, and [Jesus] was God. [Jesus] was in the beginning with God. All things came into being through [Jesus], and without [Jesus] not one thing came into being. What has come into being in [Jesus] was life, and the life was the light of all people ... And [Jesus] became flesh and lived among us, and we have seen [Jesus'] glory, the glory as of a father's only son, full of grace and truth. (John 1:1-4 & 14)

So, today when we celebrate the solemnity of Mary, the *Theotokos* (God-Bearer), we confess that the One who is the Alpha and the Omega, the One who is from eternity, the One who created everything, the One who rested in the womb of Mary and took flesh is fully Divine and fully human as the Catechism of the Catholic Church says:

> The unique and altogether singular event of the Incarnation of the Son of God does not mean that Jesus Christ is part God and part man, nor does it imply that he is the result of a confused mixture of the divine and the human. *He became truly man while remaining truly God.* Jesus Christ is true God and true man. Catechism of the Catholic Church 464 - emphasis added

Hence, celebrating the solemnity of the *Theotokos* is celebrating the mystery of the Incarnation, wherein Jesus became flesh and lived among us. Therefore, when the shepherds came to see Jesus, they found Mary beside Him. As St. John Eudes would say, "The heart of Jesus is the heart of Mary, and the heart of Mary is the heart of Jesus." Therefore, whenever we Catholics turn towards Mary, we turn and look at Jesus through the eyes of Mary and ponder with Mary. That is how Jesus was placed in the womb of Mary (Luke 1:26-36); that is how both Joseph and Elizabeth accepted Jesus when Mary carried Him in her womb (Matthew 1:18-25 & Luke 1:41); and that is how the shepherds and the Magi came to adore her only Son, the Savior of the world (Luke 2:8-20 & Matthew 2:9-12). May Mary, the *Theotokos* (God-Bearer), intercede for us, so that through her eyes, we can see Jesus Christ as fully Divine and fully human, living among us to give us the gift of salvation.

# Reflect and Journal

# About Saint John Eudes

Born in France on November 14, 1601, St. John Eudes' life spanned the "Great Century." The Age of Discovery had revolutionized technology and exploration; the Council of Trent initiated a much-needed reform in the Church; among the common people, it was the dawn of a golden age of sanctity and mystic fervor.

### His Spiritual Heritage

No fewer than seven Doctors of the Church had lived in the previous century. Great reformers like St. Francis de Sales, St. Teresa of Avila, and St. John of the Cross had left an indelible mark on the Catholic faith. Their influence was still fresh, as St. John Eudes came onto the scene.

He was educated by the Jesuits in rural Normandy. He was ordained into the Oratory of Jesus and Mary, a society of priests which had just been founded on the model of St. Philip Neri's Oratory in Rome. The founder was Cardinal Pierre de Bérulle, a man renowned for his holiness and named "the apostle of the Incarnate Word" by Pope Urban VII. Rounding out St. John Eudes' heritage is the influence of the Discalced Carmelites. His spiritual director, Cardinal Bérulle himself, had brought sisters from St. Teresa of Avila's convent to help found the Carmel in France. John Eudes would later become spiritual director to a Carmelite convent himself. Their cloister prayed constantly for his missionary activity.

## His Life of Ministry

As an avid participant in a wave of re-evangelization in France, St. John Eudes' principal apostolate was preaching parish missions. Spending anywhere from 4 to 20 weeks in each parish, he preached over 120 missions across his lifetime, always with a team of confessors providing the sacrament around the clock, and catechists meeting daily with small groups of parishioners.

Early in his priesthood, an outbreak of plague hit St. John Eudes' native region, and he rushed to provide sacraments to the dying. The risk of contagion was so great that no one else dared to approach the victims. In order to protect his Oratorian brothers from contagion, St. John Eudes took up residence in a large empty cider barrel outside of the city walls until the plague ended.

## His Foundations

During his missions he heard countless confessions himself, including those from women forced into prostitution. Realizing that they needed intense healing and support, he founded "Houses of Refuge" to help them get off the street and begin new lives. In 1641, he founded the Sisters of Our Lady of Charity of the Refuge to continue this work. They would live with the penitent women and provide them with constant support. Today, these sisters are known as the Good Shepherd Sisters, inspired by their fourth vow of zeal to go out seeking the "lost sheep." Occasionally, St. John Eudes would return to the site of a previous mission. To his dismay, he found that the fruits of the mission were consistently fading for lack of support. The crucial piece in need of change was the priesthood. At that time, the only way to be trained as a priest was through apprenticeship. The result of this training was so horribly inconsistent that the term "hocus pocus" was invented during this time to describe the corrupted Latin used by poorly trained priests during the consecration at mass. In 1643, he left the Oratory and founded the Congregation of Jesus and Mary to found a seminary. Seminary training was a radical and brand-new concept which had just been proposed by the Council of Trent.

## His Mark on the Church

At a mission in 1648, St. John Eudes celebrated the first mass in history in honor of the Heart of Mary. In 1652, he built the first church under the Immaculate Heart's patronage: the chapel of his seminary in Coutances, France. During the process of his canonization, Pope St. Pius X named St. John Eudes "the father, doctor, and apostle of liturgical devotion to the hearts of Jesus and Mary." The Heart of Jesus, because he also celebrated the first Feast of the Sacred Heart in 1672, just one year before St. Margaret Mary Alacoque had her first apparition of the Sacred Heart.

Although his Marian devotion was intense from a tender age, the primary inspiration for this feast came from St. John Eudes' theology of baptism. From the beginning of his missionary career he taught that Jesus continues His Incarnation in the life of each baptized Christian. As we give ourselves to Christ, our hands become His hands, our hearts are transformed into His heart. Mary is the ultimate exemplar of this. She gave her heart to God so completely that she and Jesus have just one heart between them. Thus, whoever sees Mary, sees Jesus, and honoring the heart of Mary is never separate from honoring the heart of Jesus.

## Doctor of the Church?

At the time of this writing, Bishops the world over have requested that the Vatican proclaim St. John Eudes as a Doctor of the Church. This would recognize his unique contribution to our understanding of the Gospel, and his exemplary holiness of life which stands out even among saints. For more information on the progress of this cause, on his writings or spirituality, or to sign up for our e-newsletter updates, contact spirituality@eudistsusa.org.

# About the Eudist Family

During his lifetime, St. John Eudes' missionary activity had three major areas of focus.

- For priests, he provided formation, education, and the spiritual support which is crucial for their role in God's plan of salvation.
- For prostitutes and others on the margins of society, he gave them a home and bound their wounds, like the Good Shepherd with his lost sheep.
- For the laity, he preached the dignity of their baptism and their responsibility to be the hands and feet of God, to continue the Incarnation.

In everything he did, he burned with the desire to be a living example of the love and mercy of God.

These are the "family values" which continue to inspire those who continue his work. To paraphrase St. Paul, John Eudes planted seeds, which others watered through the institutions he founded, and God gave the growth. Today, the family tree continues to bear fruit:

The *Congregation of Jesus and Mary* (CJM), also known as The Eudists, continues the effort to form and care for priests and other leaders within the Church. St. John Eudes called this the mission of "teaching the teachers, shepherding the shepherds, and enlightening those who are the light of the world." Continuing his efforts as a missionary preacher, Eudist priests and brothers "audaciously seek to open up new avenues for evangelization," through television, radio, and new media.

The *Religious of the Good Shepherd* (RGS) continue outreach to women in difficult situations, providing them with a deeply needed place of refuge and healing while they seek new lives. St. Mary Euphrasia drastically expanded the reach of this mission, which now operates in over 70 countries worldwide. A true heiress of St. John Eudes, St. Mary Euphrasia exhorted her sisters: "We must go after the lost sheep with no other rest than the cross, no other consolation than work, and no other thirst than for justice."

In every seminary and House of Refuge founded by St. John Eudes, he also established a *Confraternity of the Holy Heart of Jesus and Mary* for the laity, now known as the Eudist Associates. The mission he gave them was twofold: First, "To glorify the divine Hearts of Jesus and Mary... working to make them live and reign in their own hearts through diligent imitation of their virtues." Second, "To work for the salvation of souls... by practicing, according to their abilities, works of charity and mercy and by attaining numerous graces through prayer for the clergy and other apostolic laborers."

The *Little Sisters of the Poor* were an outgrowth of this confraternity. St. Jeanne Jugan was formed as a consecrated woman within the Eudist Family. She discovered the great need for love and mercy among the poor and elderly, and the mission took on a life of its own. She passed on to them the Eudist intuition that the poor are not simply recipients of charity, they provide an encounter with Charity Himself: "My little ones, never forget that the poor are Our Lord... In serving the aged, it is He Himself whom you are serving."

A more recent "sprout" on the tree was founded by Mother Antonia Brenner in Tijuana, Mexico. After raising her children in Beverly Hills and suffering through divorce, she followed God's call to become a live-in prison minister at the *La Mesa* penitentiary. The *Eudist Servants of the 11th Hour* was founded so that other women in the latter part of their lives could imitate her in "being love" to those most in need.

The example St. John Eudes set for living out the Gospel has inspired many more individuals and organizations throughout the world. For more information about the Eudist family, news on upcoming publications, or for ways to share in our mission, contact us at spirituality@eudistsusa.org.

# About the Author

Fr. Azam "Vianney" Mansha, CJM belongs to the Congregation of Jesus and Mary, also known as the Eudist Fathers. He is a Biblical theologian, mariologist, and the first Eudist priest from Pakistan. He holds a Pontifical Degree in Sacred Scripture along with degrees from the Melbourne School of Divinity, Australia and the Pontifical Urbana University, Rome. He has served as a faculty member and thesis advisor in different theological schools in the Philippines. He is currently serving at St. James/St. Leo Catholic Community in Solana Beach, CA and conducting Bible Studies and Parish Missions in several parishes of the Dioceses of San Diego & San Bernardino.

## More by This Author

If you liked this book, check out Fr. Azam's other published work! *To Jesus, Through Mary* is available on Amazon.com. It describes various stages of Fr. Azam's early vocational journey with all its Marian devotion, set in parallel with a description of St. John Eudes' Marian devotion and the saint's Mariological teaching.

www.ingramcontent.com/pod-product-compliance
Lightning Source LLC
Chambersburg PA
CBHW072158160426
43197CB00012B/2432